Contents

All words appearing in the text in bold, **like this**, are explained in the glossary.

Introduction

Welcome to the world of weird and wonderful animals! This first animal encyclopedia introduces you to a variety of animals – **bugs** and spiders, snakes and other **reptiles**, **apes** and **monkeys** and, finally, other **mammals**. Take a close-up look at some of the most fascinating creatures you could ever imagine!

Bugs and spiders

From flying beetles to hairy tarantulas, there are more **insects** and spiders in the world than any other type of animal. But how can you tell them apart? Bugs have six legs and spiders have eight legs. Spiders make webs out of silk, but bugs don't.

Apes and monkeys

Apes and monkeys belong to a group of **warm-blooded** mammals called **primates**. They are our nearest relatives. Monkeys have tails, but apes don't. Apes are usually bigger than monkeys.

Other mammals

There are more than 5,400 types of mammals, ranging from the fierce grizzly bear that lives on land to the playful seal that lives in the sea. Mammals are warm-blooded and feed their babies mothers' milk. Most mammals give birth to live young.

Snakes and other reptiles

Reptiles are **cold-blooded** animals with **scales**. Snakes, lizards and turtles are all reptiles. There are more than 6,000 different types. **Prehistoric** dinosaurs were reptiles too. But no reptiles alive today are as big as the giant dinosaurs!

Bugs and spiders

Which insect can lift 850 times its own weight?

What does a hissing cockroach sound like?

What do a tree nymph's **wings** look like?

Why do millipedes curl up into balls?

Where do praying mantises live?

Are tarantulas poisonous?

How big are cicadas?

Do stick insects **shed** their skin?

It looks like you are about to find out...

This is a **flying beetle.**

Snip! Snip!

The beetle's biting jaws work like a pair of scissors to cut up food.

Its antennae are stiff.

This is called a longhorn beetle because of the long **horn-**like **antennae** on its head. These are actually the beetle's nose and ears, used to smell and hear.

When the beetle wants to fly,
it lifts its hard front wings.
It flaps its thin back
wings up and down.

The beetle's long legs are
good for scurrying across
tree branches. They are
looking for the perfect
place to lay eggs.

Male cicadas are famous for being very noisy. They sing to attract females. Some sing SO LOUD that they can be heard more than a kilometre away!

Cicadas don't use their mouths to sing. They use drum-like body parts on their sides. They 'play' them by flexing their **muscles**.

This is a giant cicada.

The smallest cicadas are the size of your fingernail.
This one is as big as the palm of your hand!

It has two huge bulging eyes sticking out of the sides of its head.

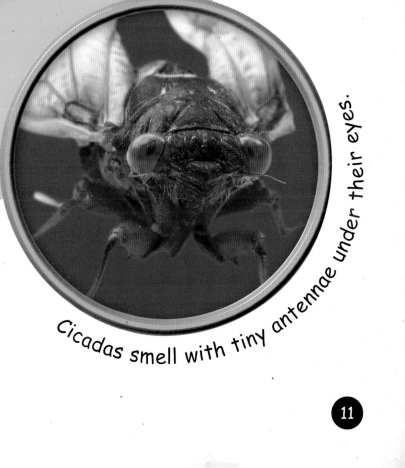

Cicadas smell with tiny antennae under their eyes.

This cicada comes from a hot and **tropical** country. That is why it has grown so big.

The name *millipede* means 'thousand legged', but most millipedes have only 300 legs. With so many legs, you'd expect them to be fast, but they are not.

Millipedes cannot see well. They use their antennae to touch and smell and to help them to find their way about.

If a millipede walked across your hand, it would tickle!

A millipede has four legs on each part of its body (centipedes have only two).

This is a millipede.

Antenna

Millipedes have hard skin like a suit of armour. They curl up into a ball at any sign of danger.

This is a **tree nymph**.

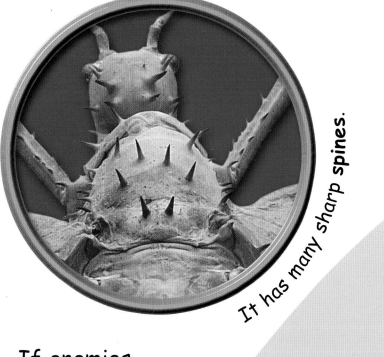

It has many sharp spines.

If enemies try to eat it, they get a mouthful of prickles!

This tree nymph is so big that you'd need two hands to hold it!

Its front wings look like leaves.
Its legs look like thorny twigs.

When a tree nymph sits in a tree and stays still, it looks like part of the tree! This is called **camouflage**.

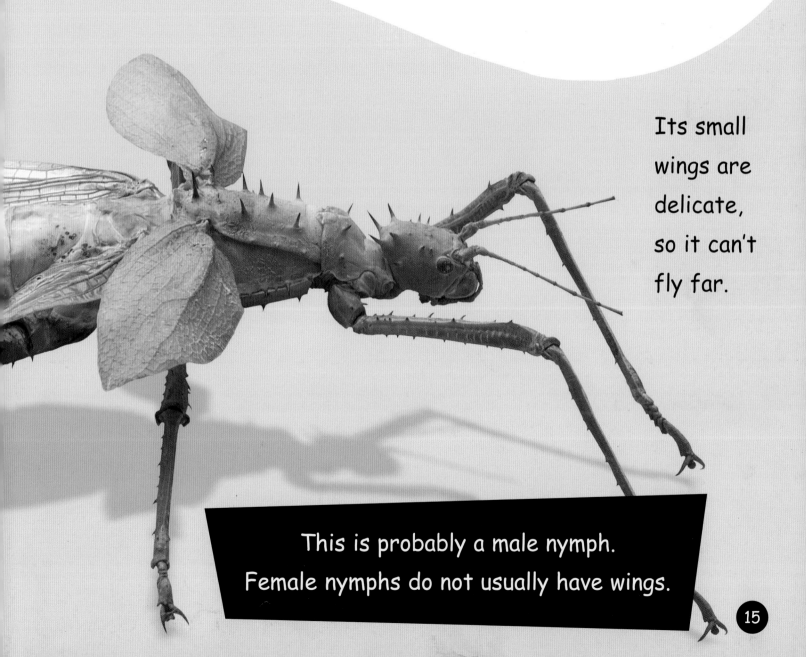

Its small wings are delicate, so it can't fly far.

This is probably a male nymph. Female nymphs do not usually have wings.

The **spikes** on its legs are for gripping and protection.

To make a hissing noise, the cockroach pushes air out of a pair of breathing holes on the sides of its body.

Hissss...

Each male has his own special hiss that can be heard up to four metres away!

This is a hissing cockroach.

Hissing cockroaches make a noise like air coming out of a tyre. They do this if they are disturbed, or to startle their enemies, such as spiders.

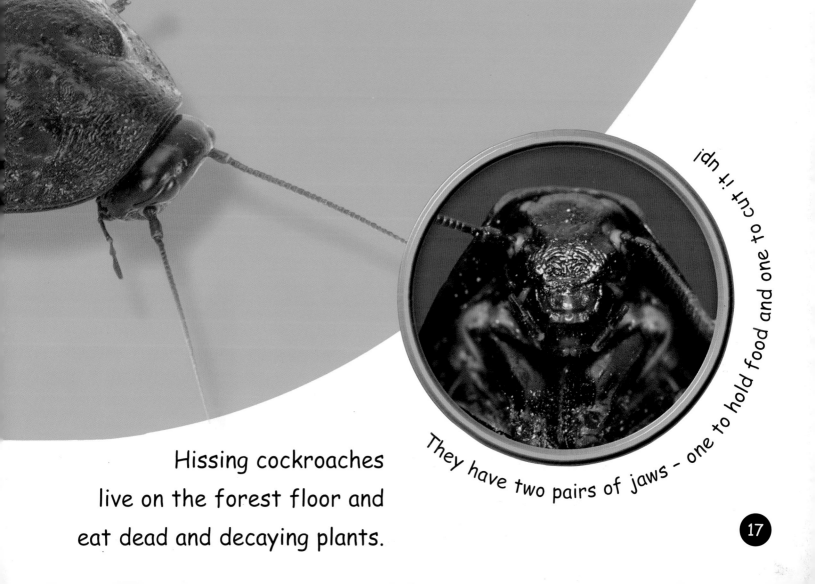

Hissing cockroaches live on the forest floor and eat dead and decaying plants.

They have two pairs of jaws – one to hold food and one to cut it up!

17

This is a tarantula.

Underneath its head are two poisonous *fangs*.

Tarantulas are usually shy and peaceful. Their bite may be poisonous, but they are not deadly.

This tarantula is only five years old.

If this spider loses a leg, it can grow another one. It takes seven years to regrow!

Tarantulas are the hairiest spiders of all.
They use their hairs to **sense** food, enemies
or mates. And if you make them angry, they
flick their stinging hairs at you!

It may live to see its 30th birthday.

Its fangs are under here.

Red-knee tarantulas,
like this one, live in the
rainforests of Mexico.
Their home is a
burrow lined
with silk.

There are eight tiny eyes on the
tarantula's head, but it can't see well.

This is a five-horned rhinoceros beetle.

Its flying wings are twice as long as its hard front wings.

Rhinoceros beetles could easily win a bug weightlifting contest. They can lift 850 times their own weight!

With five **horns**, this is the scariest of all the rhinoceros beetles. It uses its horns for digging or fighting with other males.

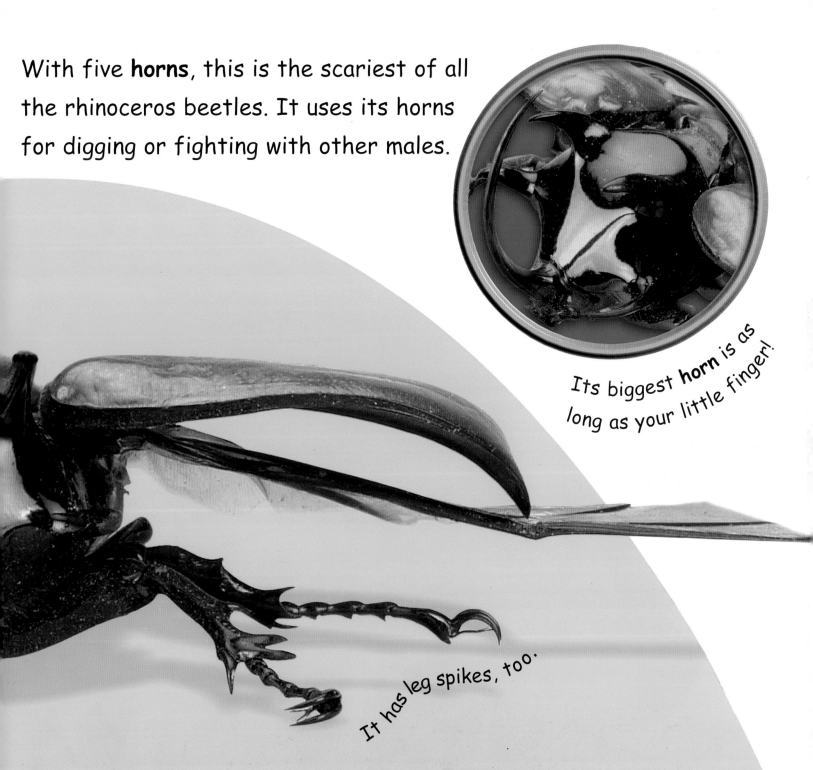

Its biggest **horn** is as long as your little finger!

It has leg spikes, too.

This beetle can fly long distances without eating. It uses the energy stored in its big, fat body.

This is a stick insect.

Its long body looks just like a thin brown twig. This is for camouflage.

Stick insects **shed** their skin, just like snakes.

The giant stick insect is the longest insect in the world. It grows up to 30 centimetres long.

Its two long antennae are used for smelling and feeling its way.

Antenna

Most of the time, stick insects stay still, which makes them very difficult to spot. But they can move fast if they need to.

Who would have thought it - stick insects have faces!

The stick insect has strong biting jaws to chew on tough leaves.

Its jaws are very powerful, for biting into live **prey**.

This is a praying mantis.

Praying mantises live in warm places, such as rainforests. They are related to cockroaches.

The mantis is a fierce and deadly hunter that eats insects and other small animals alive!

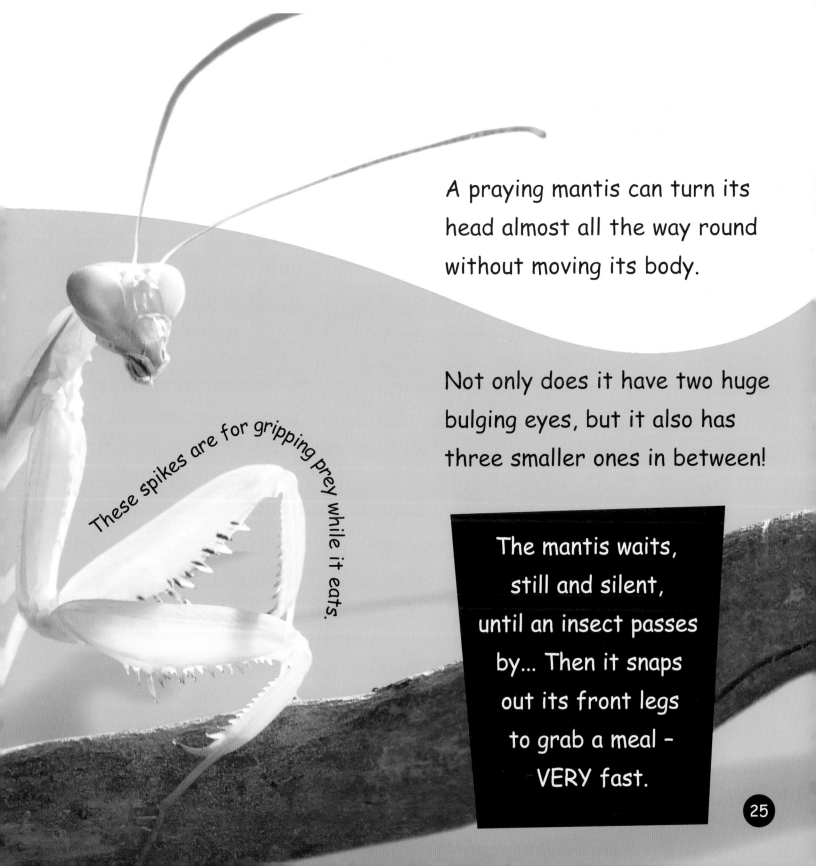

A praying mantis can turn its head almost all the way round without moving its body.

Not only does it have two huge bulging eyes, but it also has three smaller ones in between!

These spikes are for gripping prey while it eats.

The mantis waits, still and silent, until an insect passes by... Then it snaps out its front legs to grab a meal – VERY fast.

Snakes and reptiles

Which is the longest **venomous** snake in the world?

Where do baby crocodiles hide to stay safe?

What is the thorny devil's favourite food?

Why are hawksbill turtles **endangered**?

Can chameleons change colour?

Where do rattlesnakes live?

Do gaboon vipers eat often?

How many toes does the bearded dragon have on each foot?

How do pythons kill prey?

Are snakes slimy?

It looks like you are about to find out...

27

Snakes can't see very well. They track small animals by smell.

A hungry python grabs its prey with its teeth and then loops its body in coils round the meal.

The snake squeezes hard, **suffocating** the prey to death.

The python's mouth can open wide enough to swallow an animal bigger than its own head!

28

This is a royal python.

This African royal python is about 1.5 metres long. The longest pythons grow to a length of eight metres!

The python swallows its prey whole. This can take one hour, but one good meal lasts the python for weeks.

This is a corn snake.

Corn snakes are also called rat snakes because they eat rats and mice. Some people are scared of snakes, but this one can't hurt people. It is not poisonous to humans.

A snake has no eyelids.

Its eyes are always open — even when it is asleep!

Snakes flick their tongues out to 'taste' the air and see if they can sense a meal nearby.

Snakes have Y-shaped tongues.

Corn snakes can grow up to 1.5 metres long.

Some people
keep corn snakes
as pets.

Snakes are not slimy to touch.
Their skin feels dry.

A corn snake lays its
eggs in piles of rotting
leaves. This keeps
the eggs warm. After
60 days of **incubation**,
baby snakes wriggle out
of the eggs and start
hunting for food.

When a rattlesnake hears something coming, it lifts up the tip of its tail and rattles it as a warning.

The hard scales of the rattle click together.

Rattle, rattle!

Rattlesnakes weigh up to 15 kilograms.

Like all snakes, a rattlesnake sheds its skin as it grows. It does this two or three times a year.

This is a rattlesnake.

Rattlesnakes live in hot **deserts** and hardly ever drink water. This diamondback rattlesnake grows up to two metres in length.

A rattlesnake kills with poison from its fangs. Snake poison is called venom.

Most rattlesnakes give birth to live babies – sometimes as many as 50.

33

Vipers are not big eaters. A gaboon viper in a zoo once went for more than two years without eating!

The viper has the longest fangs of any venomous snake. They fold back into its top jaw. When it opens wide to bite, the fangs swing forwards.

It is one of the deadliest poisonous snakes.

The fangs pump venom into the prey and kill it in seconds.

This is a gaboon viper.

The gaboon viper lives in Africa. Its skin pattern helps the snake to hide among the forest leaves. This is a form of **camouflage**.

The gaboon viper is quite lazy and likes to stay hidden away. So, luckily, it hardly ever bites people!

It has heat-sensitive pits in its lip scales.

Its fangs are more than three centimetres long.

The gaboon viper's heat-sensitive pits sense the viper's prey in the dark.

This is a cobra.

Cobras are the longest venomous snakes in the world. The king cobra of Asia can grow to four metres long. Some cobras can spit venom and hit an enemy two metres away. The poison blinds the enemy while the snake wriggles to safety.

A cobra has a hood of skin behind its head. The markings look like a face. When it meets an enemy, the snake rears up and spreads out its hood.

The snake's markings help to camouflage it among the leaves and twigs of the forest where it lives.

The hood makes the cobra look bigger than it really is.

Cobras eat small animals, including birds, lizards and toads. They even eat other snakes!

This is a chameleon.

Chameleons are lizards – reptiles that have legs and tails. They move very slowly, lifting one foot at a time.

It swivels its eyes to look all around.

Chameleons can see forwards with one eye and backwards with the other eye – at the same time!

Its tongue is longer than its body!

To catch insects, spiders and smaller lizards, the chameleon shoots out its tongue at lightning speed – too fast to see! On the tip of the tongue is a sticky blob that catches the meal.

It hangs onto a branch with its claws and strong tail.

Chameleons can change colour. This happens when the temperature or amount of light changes. It can also happen if the chameleon gets scared or excited.

Special skin cells change the colour of the chameleon's skin.

39

It eats ants one at a time...

...so eating dinner takes forever!

This lizard loves to eat ants. It waits for a queue of ants to march past, then licks them up with its tongue.

This lizard can eat 1,000 ants in a single meal!

Like cactus plants, these lizards are prickly all over.

Thorny devils can grow up to 20 centimetres long.

This is a thorny devil.

Thorny devils live in Australia's hot deserts. Like all reptiles, they are **cold-blooded** and have to warm up in sunshine. If the afternoon sun gets too hot, they cool off under a shady rock.

The thorns help the lizard to catch water.

Dew forms on the lizard's back at night and trickles along the prickly path into its mouth. Then the lizard has a drink.

This is a bearded dragon.

This lizard lives in Australia. Lizards are always alert. They may look sleepy basking in the sun, but in an instant they can scuttle away.

Look - a frilly beard!

The lizard's beard is a frill of skin. The male can spread the frill to make himself look bigger. This impresses female lizards and startles enemies.

All reptiles have scaly skin. The bearded dragon's feet are covered in scales, just like the rest of its body.

Some lizards do not have legs, so they look like snakes. But the bearded dragon has legs, with five toes on each foot.

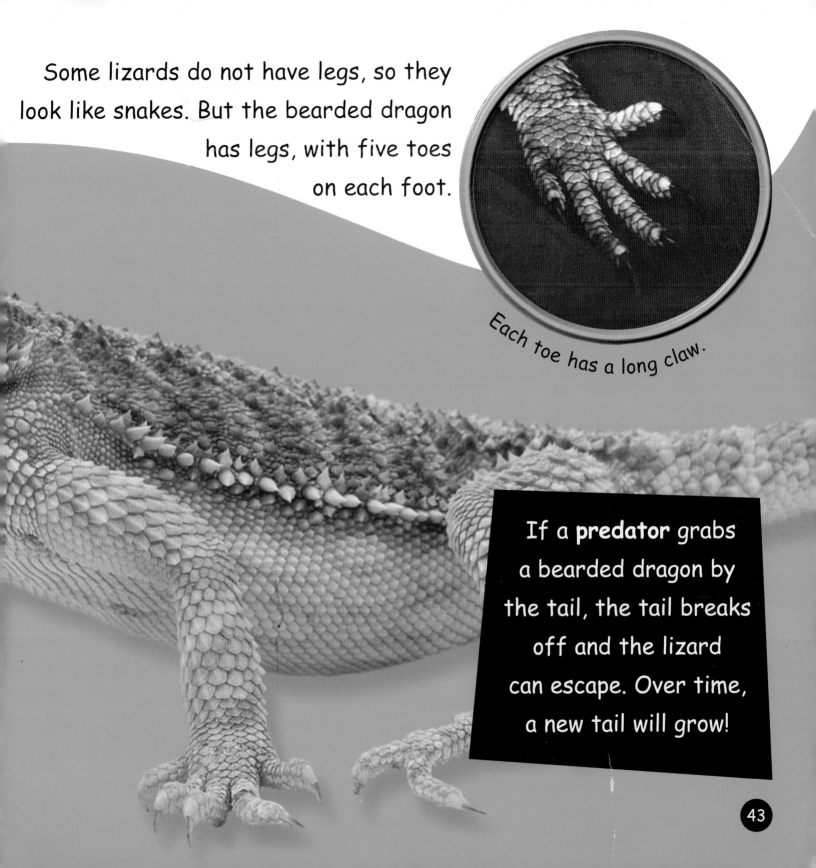

Each toe has a long claw.

If a **predator** grabs a bearded dragon by the tail, the tail breaks off and the lizard can escape. Over time, a new tail will grow!

This is a hawksbill turtle.

Turtles are swimming reptiles. Hawksbill turtles
live in the sea in warm, tropical
parts of the world.

To swim,
turtles wave
their front
flippers up
and down.

Turtles have shells like tortoises.

The back flippers are used for steering.

Turtles like shallow water best.
They can dive down to nibble
on sea sponges, their favourite food.

Female turtles crawl up onto a beach, dig a hole in the sand and lay their eggs. When the baby turtles hatch, they dash to the water.

The eggs have rubbery shells.

Many baby turtles are eaten by **predators** before they reach the safety of the sea.

Sea turtles are **endangered**. They get trapped in fishing nets and people hunt them for their shells. Hotels are built on the beaches where they lay their eggs.

A crocodile waits for its prey to come down to the water's edge for a drink.

Large crocodiles can catch large prey such as young hippo, buffalo and giraffes.

The crocodile lies in wait, with only its eyes above the surface of the water. Then it lunges and grabs its prey's head, pulling the animal into deeper water to drown it.

A crocodile has powerful jaws that can crush the bones of its prey.

This is a crocodile.

Crocodiles are cold-blooded. They need to lie on the riverbank in the sun in order to warm up their bodies.

Tough skin protects against enemy attacks.

To stay safe, baby crocodiles hide inside their mother's mouth.

Crocodiles have an extra see-through eyelid to protect their eyes under the water.

Apes and monkeys

Which is the biggest ape of all?

How big are ring-tailed lemurs?

How do chimpanzees use sticks?

Which monkeys make snowballs?

What colour is a mandrill's nose?

What are a baboon's cheek pouches used for?

Are gibbons good acrobats?

Where do orang-utans live?

Does the golden lion tamarin have claws or fingernails?

It looks like you are about to find out...

49

This is a gorilla.

Gorillas live in Africa. They are the biggest of all the apes. Male gorillas are much bigger and stronger than humans. Gorillas look fierce, but they are very peaceful animals.

Gorillas live in family groups. They spend their days on the ground, searching for leaves and fruits to eat. At night they build a sleeping nest from branches and leaves.

Gorillas have individual nose prints, like you have fingerprints!

Each gorilla family is led by a large male called a silverback. Silver-grey hair grows on his back. He scares away other silverbacks and animals by beating his chest and roaring.

A big male gorilla can weigh 180 kilograms.

Gorillas are endangered animals. The only real enemies that gorillas have are humans.

Newborn gorillas weigh only about three kilograms. Mothers carry their babies around until they are three months old.

This is a chimpanzee.

Chimpanzees live in Africa and are our nearest animal relatives. Chimps live in groups of up to 50 animals. They weigh around 60 kilograms and are about 1.5 metres tall. Sometimes they stand on two legs, but they walk mainly on all fours.

They have hair all over their bodies, bald faces and hairy chins!

Chimpanzees make faces to show that they are feeling angry, happy or frightened.

Baby chimpanzees need their mothers to do everything for them, just like human babies. They like to be cuddled, too!

Chimpanzees use sticks as **tools**. They poke the sticks into **termite** mounds. They then pull them out and lick up any termites that are clinging on. Adults teach young chimps what to do.

Chimp hands look like human hands.

Orang-utans live alone most of the time. They climb trees to look for fruits and leaves to eat.

Long, strong arms are useful for climbing trees and swinging.

Orang-utans have lots of shaggy red hair.

Orang-utans are good at solving problems. They have been seen making leaf hats to stay dry during rainstorms, and they use leaves as gloves to handle prickly fruits!

This is an orang-utan.

Orang-utans live in tropical forests on the islands of Borneo and Sumatra in southeast Asia. The name *orang-utan* means 'old man of the woods'. Today, orang-utans are endangered animals.

The males weigh up to 86 kilograms. They develop huge cheek pads. These show females that the males are strong and successful.

This is a gibbon.

Gibbons live in southeast Asia. With their very long arms, they are the acrobat stars of the forest. A gibbon can leap nine metres from one branch to another and can race through the trees at 55 kilometres per hour.

Gibbons eat fruits, leaves, flowers and seeds.

Gibbons never know where to put their long arms when they are relaxing!

Hanging about is what gibbons do best.

Gibbons stay in the trees if they can. When they come down to the ground, they run along on their back legs, their arms in the air.

56

This is the white-handed, or lar, gibbon.

The colour of their fur varies from light to dark brown, and from black to white.

Gibbons can pick things up with their feet and hands.

Gibbon families make hoot-like calls that can be heard almost three kilometres away. This warns other gibbons to stay away from their territory.

This is a baboon.

This big monkey is a baboon. As many as 150 baboons may live together in a group called a **troop**. Strong male baboons guard the troop, barking when danger is near – just like a dog!

A baboon has pouches in its cheeks for carrying food. Baboons eat almost anything. They like birds' eggs, fruits, grass, seeds, leaves and roots. They will also steal crops from farms.

Hang on tight!

Baboon babies get a ride on their mothers' backs.

The baboon has a dog-like muzzle.

These nice, even teeth can give a nasty nip!

Baboons live on the ground. They run on all fours.

A big male baboon weighs about 40 kilograms.

There are five types of baboon. This is a hamadryas baboon.

Perched up high on a rock, this baboon looks out for enemies. He doesn't scare easily and will even stand his ground against a leopard!

59

These are Japanese macaques.

Most monkeys live in warm places, such as Africa, India and South America. These Japanese macaques live in Japan, where it is cold during the winter. They need their thick fur to keep warm.

All monkeys like company. They live in family groups. The Japanese macaques eat fruits, seeds, leaves, tree buds and bark, plant shoots, flowers and sometimes crabs and grasshoppers.

Macaques have red faces with no hair.

Some Japanese macaques have learned to make snowballs.

Watch out!

Most monkeys have large eyes that face forwards. When they are climbing trees, this helps the monkeys to judge the distance from one branch to another.

On very cold days, some Japanese macaques bathe in pools of water heated by hot underground rocks. The hot water warms up their frozen toes.

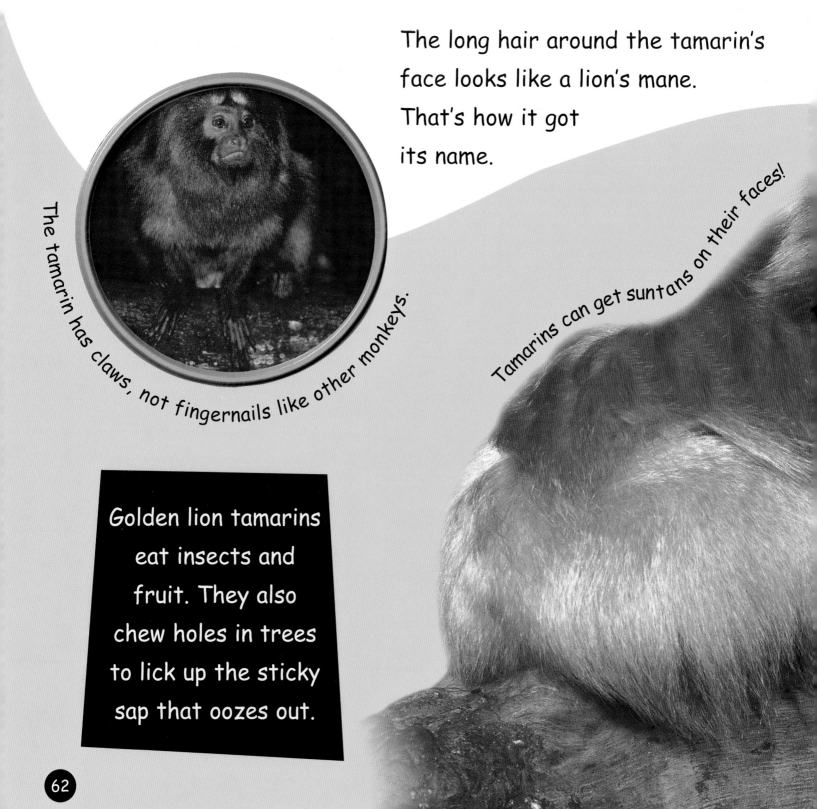

The long hair around the tamarin's face looks like a lion's mane. That's how it got its name.

The tamarin has claws, not fingernails like other monkeys.

Tamarins can get suntans on their faces!

Golden lion tamarins eat insects and fruit. They also chew holes in trees to lick up the sticky sap that oozes out.

This is a golden lion tamarin.

Tamarins are small monkeys from South America that are endangered. The forests where they live are being cut down to make room for farms. Some tamarins from zoos are taken to live in special **protected** parts of the forests.

You can tell this tamarin is a South American monkey because its nostrils point sideways. African and Asian monkeys have nostrils that point downwards, like humans.

Today, about 1,000 golden lion tamarins live in the South American forests. Twenty years ago, there were less than 600.

These are ring-tailed lemurs.

Millions of years ago, lemurs lived all around the world. Now they are found only in zoos or in the wild on the island of Madagascar. The ring-tailed lemur is the size of a cat. It has a long striped tail, which gives it its name.

Lemurs spend most of their time on the ground looking for food. They eat fruits, leaves, birds' eggs and small animals.

Held up high, this tail makes a useful 'flag'.

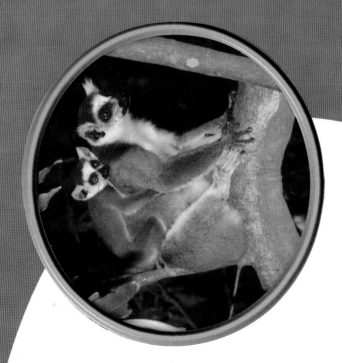

Baby lemurs ride on their mother's back until they are seven months old.

Lemurs could be in danger because people are cutting down the forests where they live.

The babies never lose their grip, even when their mother is leaping about in the trees.

These lemurs have stink fights! They wipe a smelly **scent** from special places on their wrists onto their tails and then wave the stinky tails at their opponents.

Lemurs have wet noses, like dogs.

Lemurs are not monkeys or apes – they are **prosimians**. Their main sense is smell, like dogs, not sight like apes and monkeys.

It has a stubby tail, short legs and a purple bottom!

Mandrills climb trees only at night – that's where they sleep.

A colourful face shows that the male mandrill is strong and successful. This makes him very attractive to females!

By day, mandrill families prowl round on the ground looking for food. They have strong, sharp teeth to eat fruit and seeds, and sometimes eggs and small animals.

This is a mandrill.

Mandrills live in the forests of Africa. They are the biggest of all the monkeys.

Each mandrill family defends its food supply. They chase away any other mandrill group that comes into its territory.

Mandrills are powerful animals, and they look fierce. But they are wary of strangers – especially human beings.

67

Other mammals

How do sea otters stop themselves floating away?

Do male or female lions do most of the hunting?

Which is the world's fastest land animal?

How do killer whales talk to one another?

Where are a hippo's ears, eyes and nose?

Where do grizzly bears build **dens**?

What do seals love to eat?

Are wolves good parents?

It looks like you are about to find out...

This is a grizzly bear.

The grizzly bear is the fiercest mammal in North America. Female bears are especially dangerous when they are protecting their cubs. Grizzlies can run as fast as 50 kilometres per hour – even racehorses would find it difficult to escape a rushing grizzly!

Grizzly bears are omnivores.

Their coats are usually dark brown.

They have big, powerful jaws and long claws that are the length of a human finger.

Grizzlies are experts at catching salmon.

Grizzlies have HUGE teeth!

Grizzlies need to eat a lot during the summer to build up their body fat. This helps them to survive throughout their long winter hibernation.

Grizzly bears **hibernate** for up to six months each year. They build a den on the north side of a hill where the snow stays frozen all winter long. They give birth to their cubs in the den.

Lions live in groups called **prides**. A pride usually has about 15 lions, and most of them are related. Each pride has its own territory.

A thick mane protects the male when he fights.

Male lions mark their territory with a scent. They roar to scare away other males.

Lions often hunt at night.

A lion's roar can be heard up to eight kilometres away.

This is a lion.

Lions live in Africa on grassy **plains** and in open woodlands. They work in teams to **stalk** and **ambush** their prey. Lions eat wildebeest, impala, zebras, buffalo and wild hogs (pigs).

A female lion is called a lioness.

A lioness doesn't have a mane around her neck.

Although male lions are bigger than females, it is the female lions that do most of the hunting.

This is a cheetah.

Cheetahs are the world's fastest animals on land. In order to survive, a cheetah needs to be even faster than the animals that it hunts. Cheetahs hunt fast-running animals, including gazelles, impala and wildebeest.

Cheetahs can run up to 110 kilometres per hour – as fast as a car on a motorway!

A cheetah has yellow-grey fur with dark spots.

Cheetahs cannot run at such high speeds for long. If they don't quickly catch their prey, they have to rest before they can try again.

Cheetahs have thinner bodies and longer legs than most members of the cat family.

Cheetahs have weak jaws and small teeth. If they meet a large predator, such as a lion, they run away to protect themselves.

The cheetah's fur makes it difficult to see in long grass. This is called **camouflage**, and helps it stalk its prey.

Male killer whales have the tallest dorsal fins of any animal. They can grow up to two metres high.

The dorsal fin helps the killer whale with high-speed swimming.

Killer whales live in family groups called **pods**. A pod can have between 5 and 30 members.

Killer whales talk to one another with a mixture of whistles, screams and clicks. Each pod has a slightly different language.

This is a killer whale.

The killer whale, or orca, is not a whale. It is the biggest member of the dolphin family. Killer whales have powerful bodies and many strong teeth.

Killer whales eat seabirds, turtles, fish and squid, seals, sea lions and even other dolphins and whales – almost any creature that swims or floats!

Wolves communicate by making different faces. For example, showing their teeth and pointing their ears forwards is a threat.

Wolves are good parents. The male hunts for food and then brings it back to the den. As the wolf cubs grow, the mother and other members of the pack help to feed them.

Wolves have two layers of fur to keep warm.

This is a wolf.

Wolves live and hunt in groups called packs. They have their own territory, but sometimes travel far outside it to hunt. When a pack is together, howling makes the wolves excited to hunt and helps them to keep in touch.

A wolf has long fur on the outside and short fur next to the skin.

Wolves hunt and kill prey up to ten times heavier than their own weight.

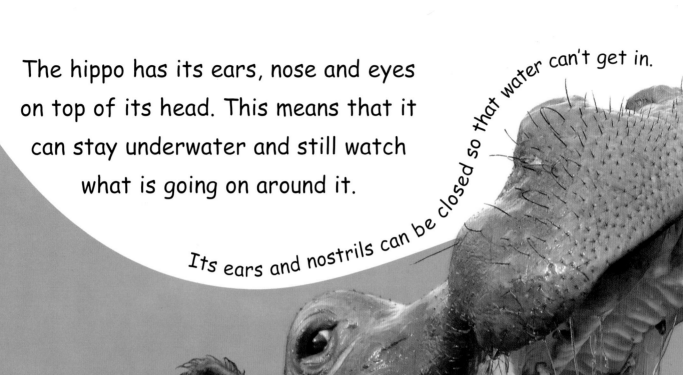

The hippo has its ears, nose and eyes on top of its head. This means that it can stay underwater and still watch what is going on around it.

Its ears and nostrils can be closed so that water can't get in.

Hippo are **herbivores** that spend most of the day resting in the rivers where they live. They can stay underwater for up to 30 minutes.

This is a hippopotamus.

Hippos look quiet and peaceful, but if something makes them angry, they can be one of the most dangerous animals in Africa.

These male hippos are fighting.

Who has the scariest mouth?

Males have huge teeth that can grow up to 70 centimetres long.

A hippo can bite a three-metre-long crocodile in half. It can also reach a top speed of 32 kilometres per hour on land when it runs.

This is a sea otter.

Sea otters live on the west coast of the United States, between California and Alaska. They eat shellfish and other sea creatures. They float on their backs with the shellfish balanced on their stomach. Then they hammer with a stone until the shell breaks.

Otters have special flaps of skin under their front paws that help them to hold onto food.

Sea otters close their ears and noses when they are under the water.

An otter enjoys a delicious shrimp dinner!

To stop themselves from floating away, sea otters wrap long strings of kelp (a type of seaweed) round their bodies.

Sea otters love to float. They even sleep floating on their backs!

Their back legs are shaped like flippers – this helps otters to swim.

83

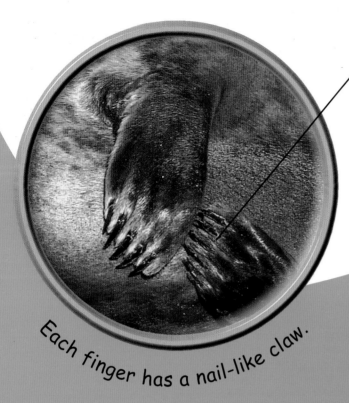

These are the seal's front feet, or flippers. Although the 'fingers' are joined together to make swimming easier, you can see them clearly.

Each finger has a nail-like claw.

Seal milk is packed with goodness. When seal pups are born, they weigh about seven kilograms. Only 12 days later, they can weigh 35 kilograms!

The back flippers are **webbed**, and seals have to shuffle along slowly on land.

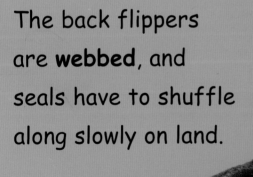

This is a seal.

Most types of seal live in cold places. Their bodies have a thick layer of fat called blubber to keep them warm. Seals love to eat fish, shellfish, shrimp, octopuses and squid.

Seals have lots of warm **blubber**.

The whiskers are used to detect fish prey.

Did you know?

Here are some more weird and wonderful animal facts:

- Dung beetles can roll a ball of dung 50 times their own weight.

- During the winter, ladybirds hibernate under logs, leaves or bark.

- A bee may fly up to 100 kilometres in one day searching for food.

- Houseflies use their feet to 'taste'.

- If a gecko's tail breaks off, the tail keeps on wriggling.

- The deadly komodo dragon can smell food ten kilometres away.

- A Galápagos tortoise can live to be 150 years old.

- Alligators have up to 60 teeth.

- The siamang, a type of ape, has two fingers on each hand that are fused together.

- During the mosquito season, capuchin monkeys rub crushed millipedes onto their backs to deter the insects.

- Pygmy marmosets are only about 15 centimetres tall when they reach full size.

- The call of a howler monkey can be heard five kilometres away in the rainforest.

- A camel can survive without water for nearly two weeks.

- Elephant calves weigh more than 100 kilograms when they are born.

- Polar bears' paws are the size of dinner plates.

- Every zebra has a different pattern of stripes.

GLOSSARY

ambush To attack prey from a hidden position.

antennae Organs on the heads of some insects that are used to sense things around them.

apes A primate that has no tail but has a big brain. Gorillas, orang-utans, chimpanzees and gibbons are all apes.

blubber The thick layer of fat between the skin and muscle of seals, whales and other sea animals that keeps the animal warm and stores energy.

bugs A word used to describe a group of creeping or crawling insects.

burrow A hole dug in the ground that is used as a home.

camouflage Colour or patterns on an

animal or insect that match surroundings and protect it from predators.

cells A microscopic part of an animal's body. People, animals and plants are all made of cells.

cold-blooded Describes animals that control their body temperature with outside help such as the sun. Reptiles are cold-blooded.

crops Food plants grown by farmers.

defend Protect a family and territory by fighting or scaring away other animals.

dens Animals' homes or sleeping places.

deserts Hot, dry places with very little rainfall, where not many people, animals or plants live.

endangered When there are not many of a type of animal left. The remaining animals are in danger of being hunted by humans or losing their home.

fangs Long, sharp teeth used to inject poison into, or grab, hold and tear, prey.

flippers Arms or legs that have become flattened, like paddles, and are used for swimming.

herbivores Animals such as hippos that eat only plants.

hibernate To sleep through the winter, when there is not much food available.

horn A bony projecting part on the head of an insect or animal that is used to attack other creatures.

incubation The time that an egg spends in a warm place while the animal inside grows and gets ready to hatch out.

insects A group of animals that have three parts to their bodies – a head, a thorax and an abdomen – three pairs of legs and wings.

joints The points of contact between two or more bones that allow movement.

mammals Animals with warm blood that produce milk to feed their young.

mature Fully grown.

monkeys Primate animals. Many types have tails. Baboons, macaques, tamarins and mandrills are all monkeys.

muscles The body tissues that contract and relax to move parts of the body.

omnivores Animals that eat both meat and plants.

plains Large, flat areas of land.

pod A small group of sea animals, especially dolphins, seals and whales.

predator An animal that survives by hunting, killing and eating other animals.

prehistoric Belonging to a time millions of years before people lived on Earth.

prey Animals that are hunted for food by other animals.

pride A group of lions.

primates An animal group that includes monkeys, apes and prosimians. Humans are primates too.

prosimians The animals that evolved (changed over a very long time) into modern monkeys. Ring-tailed lemurs are prosimians.

protected Describes a safe place where it is against the law to hunt animals and cut down trees.

rainforests A tropical forest that has a high level of rainfall.

reptiles Animals that include snakes, turtles, lizards, crocodiles and alligators. They are cold-blooded, have scaly skin and live in warm places.

sap The sticky juice found inside trees and other plants.

scales Tough, flat sections of skin that protect the bodies of reptiles and fish.

scent A special smell left by an animal.

sense To find out about something by using senses. Most people and animals have five senses: sight, smell, hearing, touch and taste.

shed To cast off skin or hair.

spikes Pointed objects on an animal's body that are used for defence.

spines Sharp, rigid parts of an animal's body that are used for defence.

stalk To follow something without being seen in order to catch and eat it.

suffocating Stopping something from breathing.

termite An insect that lives in huge colonies (groups). Termites build large, mountain-shaped nests.

territory The area that one animal defends against other animals to keep its food supply and family safe.

tools Objects used by people and sometimes animals to help them to do a particular job.

troop A group of baboons.

tropical Describes a place where it is hot and humid with many rainforests.

venom Poison made in special glands (parts of the body) in some animals.

warm-blooded Describes an animal that is able to keep a steady body temperature, whatever the temperature of its surroundings. Mammals are warm-blooded.

webbed Webbed feet have skin between the toes to help with swimming.

INDEX